About the Author

Mr. Sagar Salunke has 10 years of experience in automation testing including QTP(UFT) and Selenium Webdriver. He has worked on large investment banking projects in tier-1 Software Companies in India, USA and Switzerland.

He has designed automation frameworks in Selenium with Java that is widely used in the IT industry.

His hobbies include travelling, watching cricket and learning latest technological stuff.

A note of Thanks to My Wife

I would like to dedicate this book to my loving wife Priyanka for loving me so much and helping me write this book. Without her support, this book would not have been a reality.

Preface

This book contains all major concepts of selenium webdriver in Java like identification of web elements using xpath, css, id, name etc.

Book also covers how to work with common web controls like editboxes , comboboxes, checkboxes with selenium in Java.

All methods of the synchronization are discussed along with examples. It also covers how we can work with multiple windows, alerts and frames.

In the end, book covers the topic of keword driven automation framework in selenium webdriver using Java.

Table of Contents

1. SELENIUM Basics

In this chapter you will get familiar with selenium Webdriver. You will also learn about the Installation of Jdk and Eclipse along with Selenium Webdriver.We will also write a simple Java program in Eclipse

1.1. What is Selenium?

Selenium is the open source web application testing framework released under apache license. Selenium can be installed on all platforms like

1. Windows
2. Linux
3. Macintosh.

It supports programming in many languages as mentioned below.

1. Java
2. .Net
3. PHP
4. Ruby
5. Python
6. Perl
7. Javascript

1.2. What is selenium webdriver?

Selenium WebDriver is the successor to Selenium RC. In earlier versions of selenium we needed Selenium RC server to execute the test scripts.

Now we can use webdriver to execute the test on particular browser. For each browser we have a separate web driver which accepts the selenium commands and drives the browser under test.

1.3. Browsers supported by Selenium.

Below is the list of browsers supported by the selenium webdriver.

1. Internet Explorer
2. Google Chrome
3. Firefox
4. Opera
5. Safari

Please note that for each browser, there is a separate web driver implementation.

1.4. Choosing technology for selenium.

As mentioned earlier, there are lot of languages that can be used for selenium scripting. Choosing the language depends upon the below factors.

1. Skill Set of employees in the organisation.
2. Training required on specific language.

I have selected Java as a programming language for selenium scripting. So in this book you will see all examples in Java only. But the same applies to other languages with some syntactical differences.

1.5. Installing selenium with Java.

Well – Now let us understand the installation steps in selenium.

The list of Softwares you will need is given below.

1. Java JDK
2. Eclipse – Popular Java IDE
3. Selenium Java API (jar file)
   @https://code.google.com/p/selenium/downloads/list
4. Web driver for Chrome (exe file)
   @https://code.google.com/p/selenium/downloads/list

You can easily check if Java JDK is installed in windows system using command ">java –version" in command prompt.

```
C:\Users\sagar>java -version
java version "1.6.0"
Java(TM) SE Runtime Environment (build 1.6.0-b105)
Java HotSpot(TM) Client VM (build 1.6.0-b105, mixed mode, sharing)
```

Figure 1 - Java Command

If you get the output as shown in figure, that means you have already java installed in your system. But if you get error saying Java is not recognized as internal or external command, Then you will have to install jdk in your system.

To install jdk you can visit below url
http://www.oracle.com/technetwork/java/javase/downloads

To install eclipse you can visit below url
https://www.eclipse.org/downloads

You can download Most of the selenium related files at
http://docs.seleniumhq.org/download/

Name	Type
configuration	File folder
dropins	File folder
features	File folder
p2	File folder
plugins	File folder
readme	File folder
.eclipseproduct	ECLIPSEPRODUCT
artifacts.xml	XML Document
eclipse.exe	Application
eclipse.ini	Configuration sett
eclipsec.exe	Application
epl-v10.html	Chrome HTML Do
notice.html	Chrome HTML Do

Figure 2 - Eclipse Folder Structure

After you download eclipse in zip format, you will have to unzip it. Folder structure of the eclipse after unzipping is shown in previuos figure.

To launch eclipse, you will have double click on the eclipse.exe file.

Once you have these softwares with you, You can follow below steps.

- Open Eclipse and create new Java Project.
- Create a package and class with name SampleTest in it.
- Go to project properties and select Java build path. Select libraries tab and then choose add external jar.

- Browse to the jar file you have downloaded in step 3 in first list above.
- Select apply and close

Below images will give you the idea of how to create a project in Eclipse.

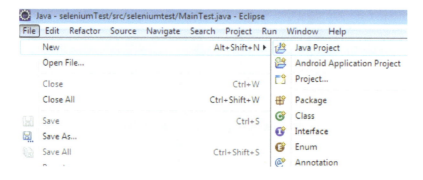

Figure 3 - Add New Java Project in Eclipse

In File menu, you have to click on new and then click on the Java Project. In new Java project window you will have to enter the name of the project and select the JRE.

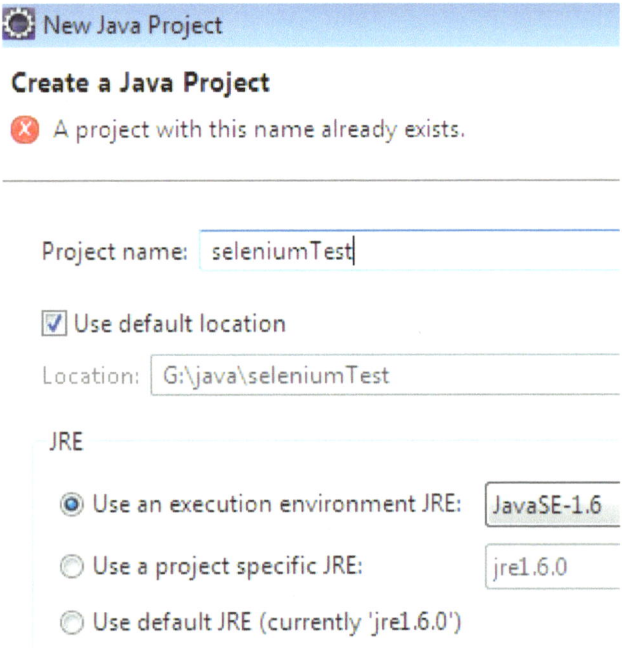

New Java Project

Create a Java Project

❌ A project with this name already exists.

Project name: seleniumTest|

☑ Use default location

Location: G:\java\seleniumTest

JRE

◉ Use an execution environment JRE: JavaSE-1.6

◯ Use a project specific JRE: jre1.6.0

◯ Use default JRE (currently 'jre1.6.0')

Figure 4 - Add new Project in Eclipse

To work with selenium webdriver, you will have to add external selenium Jar library reference by going to project properties window -> Java build path -> libraries and then click on Add external Jar. As shown in next figure, I have added selenium-server-standalone-2.35.jar library file to project.

By adding a selenium jar library file, you will be able to access the selenium classes defined in the org.openqa.selenium package and it's subpackages.

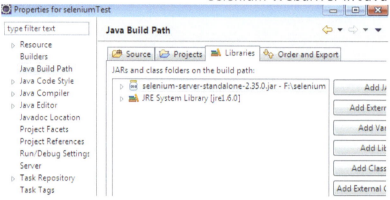

Figure 5 - Add Selenium Jar library

Next step is to create a package in the project that we have created. To add a package, right click on the folder called src under project and then select new. You will find options as shown in next image. Select package.

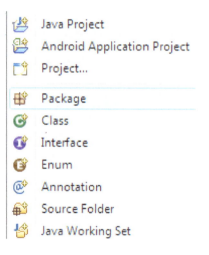

Figure 6 - Add new package

After you click on the package, you will see new package window. You will have to enter the name of package. As a convention, package names should be in small cap letters.

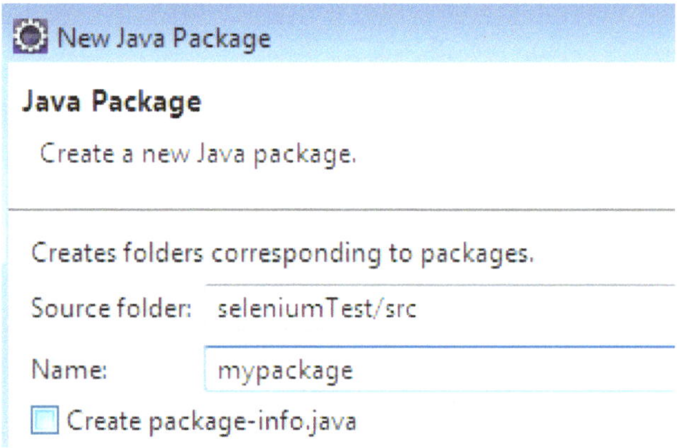

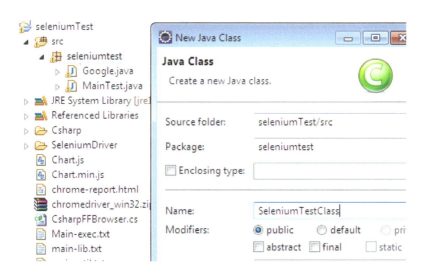

Figure 7 - Provide the name of package

Now you can add Java class, by right clicking on the package you have just added.

Figure 8 - Add new Java Class

In new Java class window, you will have to enter the name of class. As a convention, first letter of class name should be in upper case. When you click on finish, sample class code will be automatically created for you as shown in next image.

```
J *SeleniumTestClass.java ⊠

    package seleniumtest;

    public class SeleniumTestClass {

        /**
         * @param args
         */
        public static void main(String[] args) {
            // TODO Auto-generated method stub



        }

    }
```

Figure 9 - Sample Java Class Code

Now it is time to write some code in the main method and run the java program.

I have added just one line of code in the main method as shown in next figure.

System.*out*.println("First Java program in Eclipse");

Above line will print the string passed in as a parameter. To run the code, you will have to click on the run button (green ball button containing white arrow). To debug the code, you will have to click on the button looking like bug.

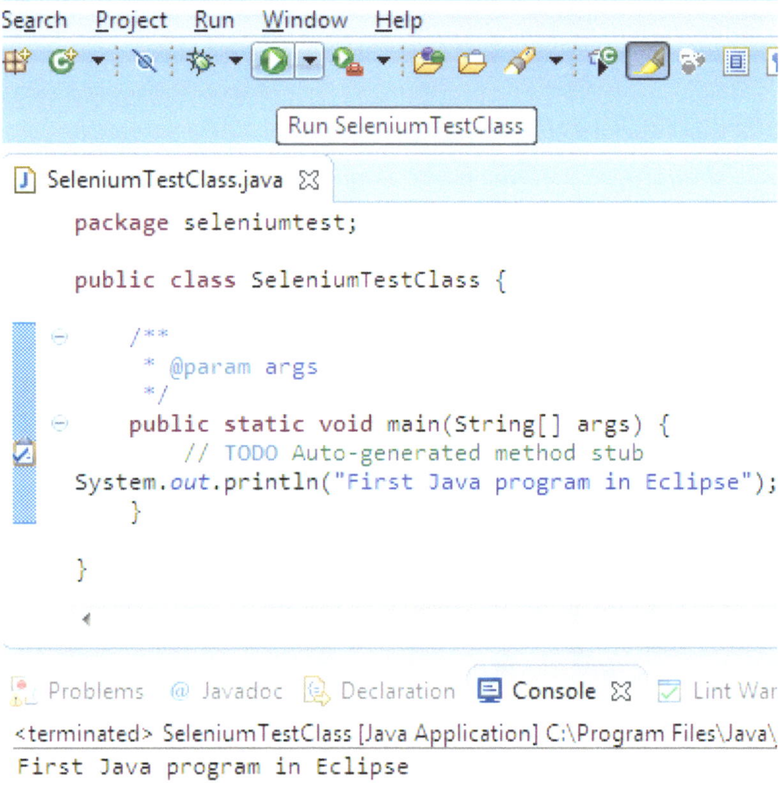

Figure 10 - Running a Java Code

After you run the program, you can see the ouput in the console window.

2. First Script in Selenium Webdriver

In this chapter, you will learn how to inspect the web elements in different browsers like IE, Firefox, Google Chrome etc. You will also learn how to write a simple selenium program in Java.

Before I jump to first script in selenium webdriver, let me explain you how you can use developer tools provided by browsers like IE, chrome, firefox while automating the web applications.

Inspecting Elements in Google Chrome.

Google chrome provides very nice tool to inspect the elements on the webpage. You have to just right click on the web element and then select last menu item from the context menu – Inspect. After you click on it, You will see the source code of that element as displayed in below image.

When you take your mouse over the html source code, corresponding element on the web page is also highlighted. This helps us to know all the values of the attributes of the element.

In next figure, we have inspected the editbox called full name at the url
http://register.rediff.com/register/register.php

The corresposning html source code is

```
<input type="text" onblur="fieldTrack(this);"
name="name" value="" style="width:185px;"
maxlength="61">
```

So for the full name editbox, we have below attributes and values.

1. type = text
2. onblur=fieldTrack(this);
3. name=name
4. value=
5. style=width:185px;
6. maxlength=61

You can use this information to write css expressions and xpath expressions which are used to identify the elements on the webpage.

Create a Rediffmail account

Full Name	:	Undo
Choose a Rediffmail ID	:	Redo
		Cut
		Copy
Password	:	Paste
		Paste as plain text
Retype password	:	Delete
Alternate Email Address	:	

s | Network Sources Timeline Profiles Resources
`<table cellspacing="0" cellpadding="0" bo`
`eight="54" align="center" class="f14">`
▼ `<tbody>`
   ▶ `<tr>…</tr>`
   ▶ `<tr>…</tr>`
   ▼ `<tr>`
      `<td width="180">Full Name</td>`

Spell-checker options

Select all

Inspect element

Figure 11 - Inspecting Elements in Chrome

Inspecting Elements in Internet Explorer.

Internet Explorer 10 and higher provides the developer tools from wehre you can inspect the elements on the webpage. You have to click on the arrow (circled in th red) and then click on the element on the webpage as displayed in below image.

Figure 12 - Inspecting Elements in IE

Inspecting Elements in FireFox.

Inspecting elements in firefox is similar to chrome. Inspecting elements will help you knowing the attributes of the elements like name, id etc. which in turn can be used in selenium scripts.

Selenium Webdriver in Java

Figure 13 - Inspecting element in Firefox

Let us start with scripting right away. Have a look at below example.

2.1 Sample Selenium Program

```java
package temp;
//all java classes are stored in the
packages.E.g. temp
import java.util.List;
import java.util.concurrent.TimeUnit;

import org.openqa.selenium.*;
import org.openqa.selenium.chrome.*;
import
org.openqa.selenium.firefox.FirefoxDriver;
import
org.openqa.selenium.ie.InternetExplorerDriver;
import org.openqa.selenium.interactions.Action;
```

```java
import
org.openqa.selenium.interactions.Actions;
import
org.openqa.selenium.support.ui.ExpectedConditio
ns;
import org.openqa.selenium.support.ui.Select;
import
org.openqa.selenium.support.ui.WebDriverWait;


@SuppressWarnings("unused")
public class SampleTest {

public static void main(String [] arg)
{
//create new webdriver instance for firefox
WebDriver driver =  new FirefoxDriver();

try{
//set the default object synchronization
timeout
driver.manage().timeouts().implicitlyWait(20,
TimeUnit.SECONDS);

//set the default Browser Navigation timeout
driver.manage().timeouts().pageLoadTimeout(50,T
imeUnit.SECONDS);

//Navigate to www.google.com
driver.navigate().to("http://www.google.com");
}

catch(Exception e){
        System.out.println("Exception - > " +
e.toString());
        }
    finally{
            //close the driver
            driver.close();
```

```
                //quit the driver
                driver.quit();
        }
    }  //main function ends

}//class ends
```

2.2.Explaination

In above program, we have created the new instance of Web Driver for firefox. In the next statements we have set the default object synchonization timeout (20 seconds) and browser navigation timeout (50 seconds). Then we have used navigate method to open www.google.com webpage.

 At the end we have closed the browser. Please note that creating a webdriver for other browsers like internet explorer and chrome is also similar except one difference - webdriver.ie.driver system property .

In short we have created the instance of the firefox webdriver and navigated to the given url.

Below code snippets show how to create the webdriver instance for the chrome and IE.

```
System.setProperty("webdriver.ie.driver",c:\\IE
Driver.exe");

WebDriver driver =  new
InternetExplorerDriver();

System.setProperty("webdriver.ie.driver",c:\\ch
rome.exe");
```

```
WebDriver driver =  new ChromeDriver();
```

When working with Selenium Webdriver and Internet Explorer, ensure that protected mode is enabled for all zones as displayed in below figure.

Figure 14 - Enable protected mode for all Zones

You must know important classes and interfaces provided by webdriver API in Java. Here is the list of important classes/Interfaces in selenium webdriver API.

1. org.openqa.selenium.WebDriver
2. org.openqa.selenium.chrome.ChromeDriver
3. org.openqa.selenium.firefox.FirefoxDriver
4. org.openqa.selenium.ie.InternetExplorerDriver
5. org.openqa.selenium.safari.SafariDriver
6. org.openqa.selenium.By
7. org.openqa.selenium.interactions.Actions
8. org.openqa.selenium.support.ui.Select
9. org.openqa.selenium.support.ui.ExpectedConditions
10. org.openqa.selenium.support.ui.WebDriverWait
11. org.openqa.selenium.TakesScreenshot
12. org.openqa.selenium.JavascriptExecutor
13. org.openqa.selenium.WebElement
14. org.openqa.selenium.Keys

3. Element identification methods in SELENIUM

In this chapter, you will learn about different methods of element identification in selenium webdriver like xpath, css, id, name, classname, tagname, linktext, partial link text.You will also come to know the difference between findElement and findElements methods.

As illustarted in the first program, It is very simple to create the webdriver instance and navigate to the webpage. In testing web application we need to perform operations on the webpage like clicking on the link or button, selecting the checkbox or radiobutton, choosing an item from the dropdown etc.

In selenium terminology, all objects in webpage are treated as webelements. So it is very important to identify the elements first and then perform some operations on them. Selenium provides plenty of methods to identify the web elements as mentioned below.

1. Xpath
2. CSS
3. Id
4. Name
5. Class Name
6. Tag Name

7. Link Text
8. Parial Link Text

We are going to look into each of these methods one by one.

Before I jump to individual identification methods, Let me explain the difference between findElement and findElements.

Well – both the methods can be used to identify the elements from the webpage. The difference is that findElement returns only single matching element while findElements returns all matching web elements from the webpage.

findElement Example

In below example, findElement method returns the first element with tag – th and prints innertext

```
WebElement we =
driver.findElement(By.tagName("th"));

System.out.println(we.getText() );
```

findElements Example

In below example, findElements method returns the collection of all elements with tag – th and prints the innertext of each one. Please note how we have used List of webelements to store all elements returned by findElements method.

```
List<WebElement> cells =
r.findElements(By.tagName("th"));

for (WebElement cell : cells) {
System.out.println(cell.getText() );
}
```

3.1 Xpath

Xpath is the web technology/standard that is used to access elements from the webpage or xml document. Detailed discussion of the xpath is beyond the scope of this book. We will see just simple examples to give you the idea of xpath. You can learn the basics of xpath at http://www.w3schools.com/xpath/xpath_syntax.asp

Examples – Suppose you want to identify the link of which href attribute contains google.

Xpath expression for above example -
//a[contains(@href,'google')]

Below code will find the first link of which **href** attribute contains google

```
WebElement we =
driver.findElement(By.xpath("//a[contains(@href,'google')]"));
```

Below table gives some sample xpath expressions.

Find all elements with tag	//input

input	
Find all input tag element having attribute type = 'hidden'	`//input[@type='hidden']`
Find all input tag element having attribute type = 'hidden' and name attribute = 'ren'	`//input[@type='hidden'][@name='ren']`
Find all input tag element with attribute type containing 'hid'	`//input[contains(@type,'hid')]`
Find all input tag element with attribute type starting with 'hid'	`//input[starts-with(@type,'hid')]`
Find all elements having innertext = 'password'	`//*[text()='Password']`
Find all td elements having innertext = 'password'	`//td[text()='Password']`
Find all next siblings of td tag having innertext = 'gender'	`//td[text()='Gender']//following-sibling::*`
Find all elements in the 2nd next sibling of td tag having innertext = 'gender'	`//td[text()='Gender']//following-sibling::*[2]//*`
Find input elements in the 2nd next sibling of td tag having innertext = 'gender'	`//td[text()='Gender']//following-sibling::*[2]//input`
Find the td which contains font element containing the text '12'	`//td[font[contains(text(),'12')]]`
Find all the preceding siblings of the td which contains font element containing the text '12'	`//td[font[contains(text(),'12')]]//preceding-sibling::*`

Below example illustrates how we can use xpath in selenium webdriver using Java. The xpath expression that we have used is -

```
//input[starts-with(@onblur,'field')]
```

Above xpath expression will identify the element with tagname as input and of which onblur attribute's value starts with **field**.

```java
package xpath;
import java.util.concurrent.TimeUnit;
import org.openqa.selenium.By;
import org.openqa.selenium.WebDriver;
import org.openqa.selenium.chrome.ChromeDriver;
import org.openqa.selenium.*;

public class Xpath {

  public static void main(String[] args) {


  System.setProperty("webdriver.chrome.driver",
"C:\\Selenuim\\chromedriver.exe");
  WebDriver driver =  new ChromeDriver();

  try{


driver.manage().timeouts().pageLoadTimeout(50,
TimeUnit.SECONDS);

driver.manage().timeouts().implicitlyWait(20,
TimeUnit.SECONDS);
```

```java
driver.get("http://www.register.rediff.com/regi
ster/register.php");


 driver.findElement(By.xpath("//input[starts-
with(@onblur,'field')]")).sendKeys("Sagar
Salunke");



   Thread.sleep(2000);


 }

 catch(Exception ex){

  System.out.println(ex.toString());

 }
 finally{

  driver.close();
  driver.quit();
 }
 }
}
```

You can also use below tools to learn xpath
  1. XPath Checker
  2. Firebug.

In google chrome, you can copy the xpath of any element very easily. Below figure shows how we can do it.

Figure 15 - Copy xpath and CSS path in Chrome

In other browsers like IE and FF also, you will find similar options in developer tools.

You can also use console window to try and test xpath and CSS expressions from the console window provided in chrome.

Q | Elements | Network Sources Timeline Profiles Resources Audits Console

```
              ▼ <td width="14">…</td>
                ▼ <td width="185">
                    <input type="text" onblur="fieldTrack(this);" name="name" value
                    style="width:185px;" maxlength="61">
                  </td>
                  <td width="6"></td>
                ▶ <td width="272">…</td>
                </tr>
              ▶ <tr> </tr>
```

html body center form div#wrapper table.f14 tbody tr td **input**

Console Search Emulation Rendering

⊘ ▽ <top frame>   ▼

```
> $x("//input[@name='name']")
  [<input type="text" onblur="fieldTrack(this);" name="name" value style="width:185px;
> $("input[name='name']");
  <input type="text" onblur="fieldTrack(this);" name="name" value style="width:185px;"
> $$("input[name='name']");
  [<input type="text" onblur="fieldTrack(this);" name="name" value style="width:185px;
>
```

Figure 16 - Console window in chrome

To test xpath expressions, you can use below syntax.
```
$x("//input[@name='name']")
```

To test CSS expressions, you can use below syntax. $ will return only first matched element.
```
$("input[name='name']")
```

To test CSS expressions, you can use below syntax. $$ will return all matched elements.
```
$$("input[name='name']")
```

3.2 CSS

CSS selectors can also be used to find the web elements in a web page. Css selectors are always prefered over xpath expressions.

You can visit

http://www.w3schools.com/cssref/css_selectors.asp to learn about css selectors.

```
WebElement we = driver.findElement(By.cssSelector("#shadow"));
We.click();
```

Above code will identify the first element having id equal to "**shadow**" and then click on it.

Below table shows commonly used css Selectors in Selenium.

Find all elements with tag input	input
Find all input tag element having attribute type = 'hidden'	input[type='hidden']
Find all input tag element having attribute type = 'hidden' and name attribute = 'ren'	input[type='hidden'][name ='ren']
Find all input tag element with attribute type containing 'hid'	input[type*='hid']
Find all input tag element with attribute type starting with 'hid'	input[type^='hid']
Find all input tag element with attribute type ending with 'den'	input[type$='den']

Below example demonstrates how we can use cssSelectors to identify the elements in Java.

The cssSelectors expression that we have used is -

input[Name='name']

Above css Selector expression will identify the element with tagname as input and of which name attribute's value is **name**.

```java
package cssSelector;
import java.util.concurrent.TimeUnit;
import org.openqa.selenium.By;
import org.openqa.selenium.WebDriver;
import org.openqa.selenium.chrome.ChromeDriver;

public class CssSelector {

  public static void main(String[] args) {


    System.setProperty("webdriver.chrome.driver",
"C:\\Selenuim\\chromedriver.exe");
    WebDriver driver =  new ChromeDriver();

    try{


driver.manage().timeouts().pageLoadTimeout(50,
TimeUnit.SECONDS);

driver.manage().timeouts().implicitlyWait(20,
TimeUnit.SECONDS);

driver.get("http://www.register.rediff.com/regi
ster/register.php");
```

```
driver.findElement(By.cssSelector("input[Name='
name']")).sendKeys("Sagar Salunke");


   Thread.sleep(2000);


  }

  catch(Exception ex){

   System.out.println(ex.toString());

  }
  finally{

   driver.close();
   driver.quit();
  }
 }

}
```

3.3 Id

This method can be used to identify any object in the web page.

Only requirement is that the object should have a id attribute associated with it.

Example – Suppose you want to click on the button having id as "next". You can use below syntax to click on the button.

```
WebElement we =
driver.findElement(By.id("next"));
```

3.4 Name

This method can be used to identify any object in the web page.

Only requirement is that the object should have a name attribute associated with it.

Example – Suppose you want to click on the button with name "submit". You can use below syntax to click on the button.

```
WebElement we =
driver.findElement(By.name("submit"));
We.click();
```

3.5 Class Name

This method can be used to identify any object in the web page.

Only requirement is that the object should have a class attribute associated with it.

Example – Suppose you want to click on the button having class as "highlight". You can use below syntax to click on the button.

```
WebElement we =
driver.findElement(By.className("highlight"));
```

3.6 Tag Name

This method can be used to identify any element in the web page with given tag.

Example – Suppose you want to click on the first link. You can use below code.

```
WebElement we =
driver.findElement(By.tagName("A"));
```

3.7 LinkText

This method can be used to identify only links in the web page.
Example – Suppose you want to click on the link "news". You can use below syntax to click on the link.

```
WebElement we =
driver.findElement(By.linkText("news"));
We.click();
```

3.8 Partial Link Text

This method can be used to identify only links in the web page.
Example – Suppose you want to click on the link with the text "google news". You can use below code.

```
WebElement we =
driver.findElement(By.partialLinkText("news"));
```

4. Performing User Actions in Selenium

> *In this chapter, you will learn how to enter the data in webpage controls like editbox, combobox and how to select controls like checkbox, radiobutton. You will also know how to click on links, buttons or any other web element using selenium webdriver in Java.*

Performing user actions involves identification of the elements on the webpage and then doing some operation like clicking on the button, entering the data in the editboxes, selecting a value from the drop down. Selenium Webdriver API in Java provides 3 important methods to enter data in web application.

1. sendKeys
2. click
3. selectByVisibleText, selectByIndex, selectByValue

4.1. Entering data in Editboxes

We can enter the data in the editboxes using sendkeys method as illustrated in the below example.

Below selenium code will open google.com website and then try to enter hello in the search box.

```java
import org.openqa.selenium.By;
import org.openqa.selenium.WebDriver;
import org.openqa.selenium.chrome.ChromeDriver;

public class first {

public static void main(String[] args) {
```

```
System.setProperty("webdriver.chrome.driver",
"C:\\SelenuimProject\\chromedriver2.3.exe");
WebDriver driver =  new ChromeDriver();

try{
      driver.get("http://www.google.com");

driver.findElement(By.xpath("//input[@name='q']
")).sendKeys("hello");

    Thread.sleep(2000);
  }

            catch(Exception ex){}
            finally{

                  driver.close();
                  driver.quit();
            }
      }

}
```

4.2.Selecting a value from the Combo boxes.

We can select the value from the dropdown using 3 different methods.

1. **selectByVisibleText** – using the actual text displayed in drop down.
2. **selectByValue** –using the value of the option
3. **selectByIndex** – using position of the item

Below example demonstrates how we can select the value from the drop down using selectByVisibleText method.

Below code will open http://www.amazon.in and select a Books value from the drop down.

```java
package temp;

import org.openqa.selenium.By;
import org.openqa.selenium.WebDriver;
import org.openqa.selenium.WebElement;
import org.openqa.selenium.chrome.ChromeDriver;
import org.openqa.selenium.support.ui.Select;

public class first {

public static void main(String[] args) {
System.setProperty("webdriver.chrome.driver",
"C:\\SelenuimProject\\chromedriver2.3.exe");

WebDriver driver =  new ChromeDriver();

try{
driver.get("http://www.amazon.in");
WebElement e =
driver.findElement(By.xpath("//*[@id='searchDro
pdownBox']"));

Select select=new Select(e);

//select the value Books from the combo box
select.selectByVisibleText("Books");

Thread.sleep(2000);
}

catch(Exception ex){
System.out.println("Exception " +
ex.getMessage());
        }
        finally{
            driver.close();
```

```
                    driver.quit();
            }
        }


}
```

4.3.Clicking on buttons

We can click on the buttons using click method as illustrated in the below example. To identify the button, you can use identification methods like id, name, css, xpath etc.

```
package temp;

import org.openqa.selenium.By;
import org.openqa.selenium.WebDriver;
import org.openqa.selenium.WebElement;
import org.openqa.selenium.chrome.ChromeDriver;
import org.openqa.selenium.support.ui.Select;

public class first {

public static void main(String[] args) {

      System.setProperty("webdriver.chrome.driv
er",
"C:\\SelenuimProject\\chromedriver2.3.exe");

      WebDriver driver =  new ChromeDriver();

try{
```

```
        driver.get("http://www.amazon.in");

WebElement e =
driver.findElement(By.xpath("//*[@id='twotabsea
rchtextbox']"));

        e.sendKeys("Selenium");

        WebElement e1 =
driver.findElement(By.xpath("//*[@id='nav-bar-
inner']/div/form/div[2]/input"));

        e1.click();

        Thread.sleep(2000);
}

catch(Exception ex){

System.out.println("Exception " +
ex.getMessage());

}
finally{
            driver.close();
            driver.quit();
            }
        }

}
```

4.4.Clicking on links

We can click on the links using click method as illustrated in the below example. To identify the links, you can use identification methods like id, name, css, xpath,linktext, partial link text etc.

```java
package temp;
import org.openqa.selenium.By;
import org.openqa.selenium.WebDriver;
import org.openqa.selenium.WebElement;
import org.openqa.selenium.chrome.ChromeDriver;
import org.openqa.selenium.support.ui.Select;

public class first {

public static void main(String[] args) {
System.setProperty("webdriver.chrome.driver",
"C:\\SelenuimProject\\chromedriver2.3.exe");

WebDriver driver =  new ChromeDriver();
try{
     driver.get("http://www.amazon.in");

     WebElement e =
driver.findElement(By.LinkText("Sell"));
          e.click();
          Thread.sleep(2000);
}
catch(Exception ex){
System.out.println("Exception " +
ex.getMessage());
}
          finally{

                  driver.close();
                  driver.quit();
          }
     }

}
```

4.5.Setting on/off checkboxes

We can first see if the checkbox is selected using isSelected method. Then using click method we can perform the operations such as selecting or deselecting the checkboxes as illustrated in the below example.

```java
package temp;

import org.openqa.selenium.By;
import org.openqa.selenium.WebDriver;
import org.openqa.selenium.WebElement;
import org.openqa.selenium.chrome.ChromeDriver;
import org.openqa.selenium.support.ui.Select;

public class first {

public static void main(String[] args) {

System.setProperty("webdriver.chrome.driver",
"C:\\SelenuimProject\\chromedriver2.3.exe");

WebDriver driver =  new ChromeDriver();

try{
driver.get("https://www.gmail.com");

WebElement e =
driver.findElement(By.xpath("//*[@id='Persisten
tCookie']")
);

if (!e.isSelected())
{
System.out.println("checkbox was not
checked.toggled");
e.click();
}
```

```
else
{
System.out.println("Checkbox was checked...now
toggled");
e.click();
}
Thread.sleep(2000);
}

catch(Exception ex){

System.out.println("Exception " +
ex.getMessage());
              }

finally{
      driver.close();
      driver.quit();
      }
      }

}
```

4.6.Selecting the radiobutton

We can select the radiobutton using click method as illustrated in the below example. Again to identify the radio button, you can use identification methods like id, name, css, xpath etc.

```
package temp;
import org.openqa.selenium.By;
import org.openqa.selenium.WebDriver;
import org.openqa.selenium.WebElement;
import org.openqa.selenium.chrome.ChromeDriver;
import org.openqa.selenium.support.ui.Select;
```

```java
public class first {

public static void main(String[] args) {
// TODO Auto-generated method stub

System.setProperty("webdriver.chrome.driver",
"C:\\SelenuimProject\\chromedriver2.3.exe");

WebDriver driver =  new ChromeDriver();

try{
driver.get("http://register.rediff.com/register
/register.php");


WebElement e =
driver.findElement(By.xpath("//*[@id='wrapper']
/table[2]/tbody/tr[21]/td[3]/input[2]"));


e.click();

Thread.sleep(2000);
}

catch(Exception ex){
System.out.println("Exception " +
ex.getMessage());
        }

finally{

                driver.close();
                driver.quit();
        }
        }

}
```

5. Reading data from webpage in Selenium

> *In this chapter, you will learn how to read the data from webpage controls like editboxes, comboboxes etc. You will also learn how to see if the elements are enabled, disabled and selected. You will also know how to read the data from table on webpage using selenium webdriver.*

Selenium API provides 2 important methods to read data from web elements.

1. **getCssValue** – gets the value of css property of the element
2. **getAttribute** – gets the value of given attribute.
3. **getText** – gets the innertext of the element.

We can also check if

1. Element is displayed using **isDisplayed** mehtod
2. Element is selected using **isSelected** method
3. Element is enabled using **isEnabled** method

```
WebElement we =
driver.findElement(By.name("login"));

String x = we.getCssValue("width");
String x = we.getAttribute("onfocus");

//returns true if element is selected
Boolean y = we.isSelected();

//returns true if element is displayed
```

```
Boolean y = we.isDisplayed();

//returns true if element is enabled.
Boolean y = we.isEnabled();
```

5.1.Reading data from Editboxes

We can get the data from editbox using 2 methods getText and getAttribute methods as illustrated in the below example.

In below code, we have entered a value – "sagar" in the editbox with name – **name** Then using getAttribute method, we have read the value entered in the same editbox.

```java
package temp;
import org.openqa.selenium.By;
import org.openqa.selenium.WebDriver;
import org.openqa.selenium.WebElement;
import org.openqa.selenium.chrome.ChromeDriver;
import org.openqa.selenium.support.ui.Select;

public class first {

public static void main(String[] args) {
// TODO Auto-generated method stub

System.setProperty("webdriver.chrome.driver",
"C:\\SelenuimProject\\chromedriver2.3.exe");
WebDriver driver =  new ChromeDriver();

try{
driver.get("http://register.rediff.com/register
/register.php");

WebElement e =
driver.findElement(By.name("name"));
```

```
e.sendKeys("sagar");


String actualValue = e.getAttribute("value");

System.out.println(actualValue);

Thread.sleep(2000);
}

catch(Exception ex){
System.out.println("Exception " +
ex.getMessage());
        }
finally{


                driver.close();
                driver.quit();
        }
    }

}
```

5.2.Reading data from combo boxes

We can get the data from combobox using 2 methods getText and getAttribute methods as illustrated in the below example.

```
package temp;
import org.openqa.selenium.By;
import org.openqa.selenium.WebDriver;
import org.openqa.selenium.WebElement;
import org.openqa.selenium.chrome.ChromeDriver;
import org.openqa.selenium.support.ui.Select;
```

```java
public class first {

public static void main(String[] args) {
            // TODO Auto-generated method stub

System.setProperty("webdriver.chrome.driver",
"C:\\SelenuimProject\\chromedriver2.3.exe");
WebDriver driver =  new ChromeDriver();

try{
driver.get("http://register.rediff.com/register
/register.php");


WebElement e =
driver.findElement(By.name("DOB_Day"));

Select comboBox = new Select(e);

comboBox.selectByIndex(3);

String actualValue =
comboBox.getFirstSelectedOption().getAttribute(
"value");

System.out.println(actualValue);

Thread.sleep(2000);
}

catch(Exception ex){
System.out.println("Exception " +
ex.getMessage());
            }
finally{

                driver.close();
                driver.quit();

}
}
```

```
}
```

5.3.Reading data from checkboxes

We can see if the checkbox is selected or not using isSelected as illustrated in the below example.

```java
package temp;
import org.openqa.selenium.By;
import org.openqa.selenium.WebDriver;
import org.openqa.selenium.WebElement;
import org.openqa.selenium.chrome.ChromeDriver;
import org.openqa.selenium.support.ui.Select;

public class first {

public static void main(String[] args) {
            // TODO Auto-generated method stub

System.setProperty("webdriver.chrome.driver",
"C:\\SelenuimProject\\chromedriver2.3.exe");
WebDriver driver =  new ChromeDriver();

try{
driver.get("http://register.rediff.com/register
/register.php");

Thread.sleep(2000);
WebElement e =
driver.findElement(By.name("chk_altemail"));

boolean actualValue = e.isSelected();

if (actualValue)
```

```java
        System.out.println("Checkbox is
checked");
else
        System.out.println("Checkbox is not
checked");

Thread.sleep(2000);


}

catch(Exception ex){
        System.out.println("Exception " +
ex.getMessage());
                }
                finally{

                        driver.close();
                        driver.quit();
                }
        }

}
```

5.4.Reading data from Radio Buttons

We can see if the radiobutton is selected or not using isSelected as illustrated in the below example.

```java
package temp;
import java.util.List;
import org.openqa.selenium.By;
import org.openqa.selenium.WebDriver;
import org.openqa.selenium.WebElement;
import org.openqa.selenium.chrome.ChromeDriver;

public class first {
```

```java
public static void main(String[] args) {
            // TODO Auto-generated method stub

System.setProperty("webdriver.chrome.driver",
"C:\\SelenuimProject\\chromedriver2.3.exe");
WebDriver driver =  new ChromeDriver();

try{
driver.get("http://register.rediff.com/register
/register.php");

Thread.sleep(2000);
List <WebElement> le =
driver.findElements(By.name("gender"));
int i=0;

for (i =0;i<le.size();i++)
{
      if (le.get(i).isSelected())
            break;

}

String actualValue =
le.get(i).getAttribute("value");


      System.out.println(actualValue);

      Thread.sleep(2000);

}

catch(Exception ex){
System.out.println("Exception " +
ex.getMessage());
            }
            finally{
```

```
                    driver.close();
                    driver.quit();
            }
        }
}
```

5.5.Working with Tables in SELENIUM

Reading the data from the table is very easy in selenium webdriver.

We can identify the table using name, Id or xpath and then we can access the rows one by one using findElements method.

For example – In below statement will find all row elements from the given table. Please note that t stands for the table object you have found using findElement method.

```
List<WebElement> rows = t.findElements(By.tagName("tr"));
```

Another example – Below example illustrates how we can find the column number for the given column name in a table.

```
int getColumnNumber(WebElement r, String
columnName )
{

List<WebElement> cells =
r.findElements(By.tagName("th"));
int c = 0;
```

```
for (WebElement cell : cells) {
  c=c+1;
System.out.println(c + " --> "+
cell.getText() );
  if (columnName.equals(cell.getText()))
break;
}


return c;
}
```

Another example – Below example illustrates how we can check if the value in given cell matches the desired value.

Below function takes 3 parameters. First parameter is row element. Second parameter is the column number and third parameter is expected value.

```
boolean verifyValue (WebElement r, int a,
String expValue)
{
List<WebElement> mcells =
r.findElements(By.tagName("td"));
int c = 0;

for (WebElement cell : mcells) {
c=c+1;
if (c==a)
{

//we can get the value inside cell using
getText() method.

if (expValue.equals(cell.getText()))
return true;
}
```

```
   }
   return false;

}
```

6. Synchronization in SELENIUM

In this chapter, you will learn how to add synchronization points in your selenium program using various methods. You will also know how to add explicit wait conditions.

We can use below synchronization methods in selenium.

6.1 Page Load Synchrnoization

We can set the default page navigation timeout. Below statement will set the navigation timeout as 50. This means that selenium script will wait for maximum 50 seconds for page to load. If page does not load within 50 seconds, it will throw an exception.

```
driver.manage().timeouts().pageLoadTimeout(50,T
imeUnit.SECONDS);
```

6.2 Element Synchronization

We can set the default element existance timeout. Below statement will set the default object synchronization timeout as 20. This means that selenium script will wait for maximum 20 seconds for element to exist. If Web element does not exist within 20 seconds, it will throw an exception.

```
driver.manage().timeouts().implicitlyWait(20,
TimeUnit.SECONDS);
```

6.3 Script Synchronization

We can set the default timeout for the java script execution also using below syntax.

```
driver.manage().timeouts().setScriptTimeout(20,
TimeUnit.SECONDS);
```

6.3.Synchronization based upon specific condition

Synchronization methods we have discussed so far are called as implicit methods. These methods are applicable to all elements on the webpage.

Now we are going to have a look at explicit synchronization method. We can insert explicit synchronization points in the script using WebDriverWait class. Please remember that you have to import this class before you use it.

```
import org.openqa.selenium.support.ui.WebDriverWait;

import
org.openqa.selenium.support.ui.ExpectedConditions;
```

We can instruct selenium to wait until specific element is in expected condition. For example – in below code, code will wait until element with id – x becomes visible.

```
//create WebDriverWait object

WebDriverWait w = new
WebDriverWait(driver,20);

//add exceptions to ignore
```

```
w.ignoring(NoSuchElementException.class);

WebElement P = null;
//below statement will wait until element
becomes visible

P=w.until(ExpectedConditions.visibilityOfEl
ementLocated(By.id("x")));

//below statement will wait until element
becomes clickable.
p=
w.until(ExpectedConditions.elementToBeClick
able(By.id("ss")));
```

7. Advanced Operations in Selenium

In this chapter, you will learn how to perform various mouse and keyboard operatiosn like double click, right click, drag and drop etc. You will also learn how to take screenshot, how to execute javascript from selenium webdriver and how to upload a file in selenium.

7.1 Mouse and keyboard Events in SELENIUM

With Selenium webdriver's Actions class, we can perform very complex keyboard and mouse operations.

- build() : Action - Actions
- click() : Actions - Actions
- click(WebElement onElement) : Actions - Actions
- clickAndHold() : Actions - Actions
- clickAndHold(WebElement onElement) : Actions - Actions
- contextClick() : Actions - Actions
- contextClick(WebElement onElement) : Actions - Actions
- doubleClick() : Actions - Actions
- doubleClick(WebElement onElement) : Actions - Actions
- dragAndDrop(WebElement source, WebElement target) : Actions
- dragAndDropBy(WebElement source, int xOffset, int yOffset) : A(
- equals(Object obj) : boolean - Object
- getClass() : Class<?> - Object
- hashCode() : int - Object
- keyDown(Keys theKey) : Actions - Actions
- keyDown(WebElement element, Keys theKey) : Actions - Actions
- keyUp(Keys theKey) : Actions - Actions
- keyUp(WebElement element, Keys theKey) : Actions - Actions
- moveByOffset(int xOffset, int yOffset) : Actions - Actions

Figure 17 - Methods of Actions class

Please note that we need to import below classes to perform below operations.

```
import org.openqa.selenium.interactions.Action;
import org.openqa.selenium.interactions.Actions;
```

Using these methods, we can perform operations as mentioned below.

1. **ButtonReleaseAction** - Releasing a held mouse button.
2. **ClickAction** - Equivalent to `webElement.click()`
3. **ClickAndHoldAction** - Holding down the left mouse button.
4. **ContextClickAction** - opening up the contextual menu.
5. **DoubleClickAction** - double-clicking an element.
6. **KeyDownAction** - Holding down a modifier key.
7. **KeyUpAction** - Releasing a modifier key.
8. **MoveMouseAction** - Moving the mouse from its current location to another element.
9. **MoveToOffsetAction** - Moving the mouse to an offset from an element (The offset could be negative and the element could be the same element that the mouse has just moved to).
10. **SendKeysAction** - Equivalent to `webElement.sendKey(...)`

Working with Actions class involves below steps.
1. Create Actions object
2. Generate sequence of action(s)
3. Get Action
4. Perform action

```
//1.create Actions object
```

```
Actions builder = new Actions(driver);


//2.generate sequence of action(s)
builder.keyDown(Keys.CONTROL)
        .click(someElement)
        .click(someOtherElement)
        .keyUp(Keys.CONTROL);


//3. Then get the action


Action action = builder.build();


//4. execute it


    action.perform();
```

Examples -

Below code will right click on the given element.

```
package temp;
import java.io.File;
import java.util.concurrent.TimeUnit;

import org.apache.commons.io.FileUtils;
import org.openqa.selenium.By;
import org.openqa.selenium.Keys;
import org.openqa.selenium.OutputType;
import org.openqa.selenium.TakesScreenshot;
import org.openqa.selenium.WebDriver;
import org.openqa.selenium.WebElement;
import org.openqa.selenium.chrome.ChromeDriver;
import
org.openqa.selenium.firefox.FirefoxDriver;
```

```java
import org.openqa.selenium.interactions.Action;
import org.openqa.selenium.interactions.Actions;



@SuppressWarnings("unused")
public class OpenGoogle {

public static void main(String [] arg)
{

System.setProperty("webdriver.chrome.driver",
"C:\\SelenuimProject\\chromedriver2.8.exe");
WebDriver driver =  new ChromeDriver();

try{
driver.manage().timeouts().implicitlyWait(20,
TimeUnit.SECONDS);
driver.manage().timeouts().pageLoadTimeout(50,T
imeUnit.SECONDS);

driver.get("http://www.google.com/");

Thread.sleep(3000);

WebElement element =
driver.findElement(By.id("hplogo"));

Actions builder = new Actions(driver);

Action rightclick =
builder.contextClick(element).build();
rightclick.perform();


Thread.sleep(8000);


}
```

```
catch(Exception e){
      System.out.println("Exception - > " +
e.toString());
      }
      finally{
            driver.close();
            driver.quit();
      }
}     //main function ends

}//class ends
```

Below code shows how we can drag and drop elements
using selenium webdriver in Java.

```
Actions builder = new Actions(driver);

Action dragAndDropChain = builder
  .clickAndHold(someElement)
  .moveToElement(otherElement)
  .release(otherElement)
  .build();

 dragAndDropChain.perform();
```

7.2. Taking Screen shots in SELENIUM

Below code will illustrate how we can take screen shots in selenium in Java.

```java
package temp;
import java.io.File;
import java.util.concurrent.TimeUnit;

import org.apache.commons.io.FileUtils;
import org.openqa.selenium.OutputType;
import org.openqa.selenium.TakesScreenshot;
import org.openqa.selenium.WebDriver;
import org.openqa.selenium.chrome.ChromeDriver;
import
org.openqa.selenium.firefox.FirefoxDriver;

//import com.sun.jna.platform.FileUtils;


@SuppressWarnings("unused")
public class OpenGoogle {

public static void main(String [] arg)
{

System.setProperty("webdriver.chrome.driver",
"C:\\SelenuimProject\\chromedriver2.8.exe");
WebDriver driver =  new ChromeDriver();

try{
driver.manage().timeouts().implicitlyWait(20,
TimeUnit.SECONDS);
driver.manage().timeouts().pageLoadTimeout(50,T
imeUnit.SECONDS);
//driver.navigate().to("http://www.google.com")
;

driver.get("http://www.google.com/");
File scrFile =
((TakesScreenshot)driver).getScreenshotAs(Outpu
tType.FILE);

FileUtils.copyFile(scrFile, new
File("c:\\sagar\\screenshot.png"));
```

```
}

catch(Exception e){
      System.out.println("Exception - > " +
e.toString());
      }
      finally{
            driver.close();
            driver.quit();
      }
}     //main function ends

}//class ends
```

7.3 Executing Java Script in SELENIUM

We can use JavascriptExecutor interface to execute script in Selenium. It has a method called executeScript which has below prototype.

public java.lang.Object executeScript(java.lang.String script, java.lang.Object... args)

JavascriptExecutor Executes JavaScript in the context of the currently selected frame or window. The script fragment provided will be executed as the body of an anonymous function. Within the script, use document to refer to the current document.

Note that local variables will not be available once the script has finished executing, though global variables will persist. If the script has a return value (i.e. if the script contains a return statement), then the following steps will be taken:

1. For an HTML element, this method returns a WebElement
2. For a decimal, a Double is returned
3. For a non-decimal number, a Long is returned
4. For a boolean, a Boolean is returned
5. For all other cases, a String is returned.
6. For an array, return a List with each object following the rules above. We support nested lists.
7. Unless the value is null or there is no return value, in which null is returned

Arguments must be a number, a boolean, a String, WebElement, or a List of any combination of the above. An exception will be thrown if the arguments do not meet these criteria. The arguments will be made available to the JavaScript via the "arguments" magic variable, as if the function were called via "Function.apply"

Below code will illustrate how we can execute java script in selenium in Java.

We need to import below class to execute the java script in selenium.

```
import org.openqa.selenium.JavascriptExecutor;

x =  ((JavascriptExecutor)
driver).executeScript("return
document.documentElement.innerText;").toString(
);

WebElement pp
=  (WebElement)((JavascriptExecutor)
driver).executeScript("return
document.documentElement;");
```

We can execute any complex javascript code in currently loaded page using `JavascriptExecutor`.

Below code will show you how you can pass arguments to the javascript code in Selenium.

```
WebElement element = driver.findElement(By.Id("abc"));

js.executeScript("arguments[0].style.border='1px solid red';", element);
```

In above code, we have passed the webElement as an argument to java script code.

7.4 uploading files in SELENIUM

Uploading file using selenium webdriver is very simple. All you have to do is – find the input element having type attribute's value as file and then use sendKeys.

Below code will illustrate how we can upload a file using selenium webdriver in Java.

```java
package abc;
import java.util.concurrent.TimeUnit;
import org.openqa.selenium.By;
import org.openqa.selenium.WebDriver;
import org.openqa.selenium.WebElement;
import org.openqa.selenium.chrome.ChromeDriver;
public class FileUpload {

  public static void main(String[] args) {
```

```java
  System.setProperty("webdriver.chrome.driver",
"F:\\chromedriver.exe");
  WebDriver driver =  new ChromeDriver();

  try{

driver.manage().timeouts().setScriptTimeout(20,
TimeUnit.SECONDS);

driver.manage().timeouts().pageLoadTimeout(50,
TimeUnit.SECONDS);

driver.manage().timeouts().implicitlyWait(20,
TimeUnit.SECONDS);

    driver.get("http://www.xyz.com");

    WebElement uploade=
driver.findElement(By.id("uploadfile"));

// enter the file path in file input field
uploade.sendKeys("C:\\abc.docx");

Thread.sleep(2000);
    }

  catch(Exception ex){

    System.out.println(ex.toString());

    }
  finally{

    driver.close();
    driver.quit();
    }
  }

}
```

8. Working with frames and Windows in SELENIUM

> In this chapter, you will learn how to work with multiple frames, windows and alerts in selenium webdriver in Java.

All web applications involve the frames, alerts and window. Selenium webdriver provides the way to handle with alerts, frames and windows using switchTo method

8.1 Handling Frames

To work with frames we need to switch to the frame and then perform the operation inside it. Again to identify the frames, we can use any of element identification methods discussed in the beginning of the book.

```java
package seleniumtest;

import org.openqa.selenium.By;
import org.openqa.selenium.WebDriver;
import org.openqa.selenium.WebElement;
import org.openqa.selenium.chrome.ChromeDriver;
import org.openqa.selenium.firefox.FirefoxDrive
r;

public  class MainTest {

        public static void main(String[] args) {

        WebDriver driver =null;
```

```java
        System.setProperty("webdriver.chrome.dri
ver", "F:\\selenium\\csharp\\chromedriver.exe")
;

        driver = new ChromeDriver();


        try{


        driver.get("http://www.samplesite.com");



//switch to the first frame in the document


driver.switchTo().frame(0).findElement(By.id("d
d")).clear();


//switch to the frame having name =   name
WebElement e = null;

e=driver.switchTo().frame("fname").findElement(
By.id("d"));

e.clear();

//switch to the frame having id = fid
e = driver.findElement(By.id("fid"));

driver.switchTo().frame(e).findElement(By.id("d
d")).clear();

    //driver.navigate();
    //driver.navigate("http://www.google.com");

              }catch(Exception e){}
```

```
            finally{
                    driver.close();
                    driver.quit();
            }


        }
}
```

8.2 Working with Alerts

We can handle alerts using Alert Interface in Java Web Driver.

At first, we need to get the alert reference using below syntax.

```
Alert alert = driver.switchTo().alert()
```

Then we can click on Ok button using below syntax.

```
alert.accept();
```

Then we can click on Cancel button using below syntax.

```
alert.dismiss();
```

To get the text displayed in the alert, you can use getText() method

```
String text = alert.getText();
```

```
package seleniumtest;

import java.util.concurrent.TimeUnit;
```

```java
import org.openqa.selenium.*;
import org.openqa.selenium.chrome.ChromeDriver;
import
org.openqa.selenium.firefox.FirefoxDriver;

public  class MainTest {


    public static void main(String[] args) {

            WebDriver driver =null;

System.setProperty("webdriver.chrome.driver",
"F:\\selenium\\csharp\\chromedriver.exe");
            driver = new ChromeDriver();

driver.manage().timeouts().pageLoadTimeout(20,
TimeUnit.SECONDS);

driver.manage().timeouts().implicitlyWait(20,
TimeUnit.SECONDS);


                try{



    driver.get("http://register.rediff.com/re
gister/register.php");

    driver.findElement(By.name("name")).sendK
eys("ff89");


    driver.findElement(By.name("name")).sendK
eys(Keys.TAB);
                    Thread.sleep(3000);
```

```
        //driver.findElement(By.name("passwd")).c
lick();


        driver.switchTo().alert().accept();
                        Thread.sleep(4000);
                        //driver.navigate();

//driver.navigate("http://www.google.com");


            }catch(Exception e){


        System.out.println(e.toString());
                }


                finally{
                        driver.close();
                        driver.quit();
                }


        }
}
```

8.3 Working with multiple browser Windows

Below code will show you how we can handle pop up
windows in selenium in Java.

```
package temp;
import java.io.File;
import java.util.Set;
import java.util.concurrent.TimeUnit;
```

```java
import org.apache.commons.io.FileUtils;
import org.openqa.selenium.By;
import org.openqa.selenium.Keys;
import org.openqa.selenium.OutputType;
import org.openqa.selenium.TakesScreenshot;
import org.openqa.selenium.WebDriver;
import org.openqa.selenium.WebElement;
import org.openqa.selenium.chrome.ChromeDriver;
import
org.openqa.selenium.firefox.FirefoxDriver;
import org.openqa.selenium.interactions.Action;
import
org.openqa.selenium.interactions.Actions;

//import com.sun.jna.platform.FileUtils;


@SuppressWarnings("unused")
public class OpenGoogle {

public static void main(String [] arg)
{

System.setProperty("webdriver.chrome.driver",
"C:\\SelenuimProject\\chromedriver2.8.exe");
WebDriver driver =  new ChromeDriver();



try{
driver.manage().timeouts().implicitlyWait(20,
TimeUnit.SECONDS);
driver.manage().timeouts().pageLoadTimeout(50,T
imeUnit.SECONDS);
//driver.navigate().to("http://www.google.com")
;

//Please enter your web url here
driver.get("http://www.xyz.com/");
```

```java
String mainHandle = driver.getWindowHandle();

driver.findElement(By.LinkText("Open New
Window")).click();

//wait while ( driver.getWindowHandles().size()
== 1 );


Set<String> HandleSet =
driver.getWindowHandles();
//Switching to the popup window.

for ( String handle : HandleSet )
{
    if(!handle.equals(mainHandle))
    {
      //Switch to newly created window
        driver.switchTo().window(handle);
    }
}

}

catch(Exception e){
      System.out.println("Exception - > " +
e.toString());
      }
      finally{
            driver.close();
            driver.quit();
      }
}     //main function ends

}//class ends
```

9. Important Built-in Function in Java.

In this chapter, you will learn important built in classes and their methods in Java to work with strings, files, date and time, Math etc.You will need these methods when doing validations and comparisons while doing functional testing of web applications.

9.1 Working with Strings in Java

We must know below string operations while working with selenium.

```java
String x = "Sachin Tendulkar and Dhoni";

//To find the length of the string
System.out.println(x.length());

//To trim the string
System.out.println(x.trim());

//Convert the string to lower case and
upper case
System.out.println(x.toLowerCase() +
x.toUpperCase());

//Find the first n characters from left of
the string
System.out.println(x.substring(0,3));

//Find the last n characters from right of
the string
System.out.println(x.substring(x.length()-
3));
```

```java
//Find the middle characters from the
string
System.out.println(x.substring(4,7));

//replace part of string with other string
-Case-Sesitive.
System.out.println(x.replace("sachin",
"Arjun"));

//to check if the given string exists in
the another string - Case Sensitive
System.out.println(x.contains("Sachin"));

//to remove all spaces from the string
System.out.println(x.replace(" ", ""));

//to split the string use split
System.out.println(x.split(" ").length);
```

9.2 Working with Date and Time

In all banking projects, you will have to calculate the date differences or find the future or past date. So you must know how to do this in java.

```java
import java.text.*;
import java.util.*;


public class DateTime {

public static void main(String[] args)
throws Exception{

//DateFormat dateFormat = new
SimpleDateFormat("yyyy/MM/dd HH:mm:ss");
```

```java
//DateFormat dateFormat = new
SimpleDateFormat("MM/dd/yyyy");

//dateFormat = new SimpleDateFormat("dd-MM-
yyyy HH:mm");

//dateFormat = new
SimpleDateFormat("MMMMM");

//dateFormat = new
SimpleDateFormat("EEEEE");


DateFormat dateFormat = new
SimpleDateFormat("dd-MMM-yyyy");


Calendar cal = Calendar.getInstance();

System.out.println(dateFormat.format(cal.ge
tTime()));

//get future date
cal.add(Calendar.DATE, 15);
//get a date that is 15 days ahead from now
on
System.out.println(dateFormat.format(cal.ge
tTime()));

//get past date
cal.add(Calendar.DATE, -25);
System.out.println(dateFormat.format(cal.ge
tTime()));

//Compare dates
Date date1 = dateFormat.parse("2014-12-
30");
Date date2 = dateFormat.parse("2012-08-
31");
```

```
System.out.println(dateFormat.format(date1)
);
System.out.println(dateFormat.format(date2)
);


if (date1.before(date2))
System.out.println("Date1 falls before
Date2");

if (date1.after(date2))
System.out.println("Date1 falls after
Date2");

if (date1.equals(date2))
System.out.println("Date1 and Date2 fall on
same day");



}


}
```

9.3 Working with Files and Folders

Below code will create new file at given path and append
some data in it. If file already exists, it will be overwritten.

```
File temp = new File(filePath);
FileWriter fw = new FileWriter(temp,true);
fw.append(data);
fw.close();
```

9.4 Maths

Important Maths related methods provided in Java are given below.

1. Round - rounds the number to specific number of decimals.
2. Pow - to find value of x^y.

```
double x = 989.345;
DecimalFormat df=new DecimalFormat("0.00");
String formated = df.format(x);
System.out.println(Double.parseDouble(forma
ted));

//Output will be 989.34

System.out.println(Math.pow(2, 3));
```

9.5 Using Java Arrays

Arrays are used to store the multiple elements of the same type in adjacent locations.

There are mainly 2 types of arrays.

1. Native variables arrays
2. Reference Variable (object) arrays

In below example, we have array a (of integer type) and array s1 (of string type). Both the arrays are of native data types.

Third array – p is an array of objects of type
SeleniumTestClass

```java
//integer arrays
          int x =10;
//integer array declaration

          int[] a = new int[x];
//integer array initialization

          a[1] = 200;
          //int[] b = {3,4,5};
System.out.println(a.length + "--" + a[1]);



//****************************************
********

//String Arrays
//String array declaration

          String[] s1 = new String[x];

//String array initialization

          s1[1] = "selenium";
//String[] names = { "Joe", "Jane",
"Herkimer" };

System.out.println(s1.length + "--" +
s1[1]);

//****************************************
*********

//Object Arrays declaration
```

```
SeleniumTestClass[] p = new
SeleniumTestClass[2];

//Object Arrays initialization
p[0] = new SeleniumTestClass();
p[1] = new SeleniumTestClass();

//*******************************************
```

9.6 Using Java List

The java.util.List interface is a subtype of the
java.util.Collection interface. It represents an ordered list
of objects, meaning you can access the elements of a List
in a specific order, and by an index too. Please note that
you will have to import below classes while working with
lists in Java.

```
import java.util.ArrayList;
import java.util.List;
```

In below example, we have create a list y of strings and
added one value in it. We have also printed the value in
the list at position number 0.

```
//Generic List
List<String> y = new ArrayList<String>();
y.add("sagar:");
System.out.println(y.get(0).toString());
```

9.7 Regular expressions in Java

Regular expressions are used to find the matching pattern in given string. We need below classes to be able to work with regular expressions.

```java
import java.util.regex.Matcher;
import java.util.regex.Pattern;
```

```java
//Regular Expressions
String EXAMPLE_TEST = "saga 9850 amol";
Pattern pattern = Pattern.compile("\\d");

// Pattern pattern =
Pattern.compile("\\s+",
Pattern.CASE_INSENSITIVE);

Matcher matcher =
pattern.matcher(EXAMPLE_TEST);


 while (matcher.find()) {
System.out.print("Start index: " +
matcher.start());
System.out.print(" End index: " +
matcher.end() + " ");

System.out.println(matcher.group());

}
// replace digita with A
Pattern replace = Pattern.compile("\\d");

Matcher matcher2 =
replace.matcher(EXAMPLE_TEST);
```

```
System.out.println(matcher2.replaceAll("A")
);
```

```
Start index: 5 End index: 6 9
Start index: 6 End index: 7 8
Start index: 7 End index: 8 5
Start index: 8 End index: 9 0
saga AAAA amol
```

9.8 Working with databases in Java.

We can use jdbc for working with databases in Java. Below example shows how we can connect to microsoft access database in Java.

```java
try
        {

Class.forName("sun.jdbc.odbc.JdbcOdbcDriver
");
            String database =
                "jdbc:odbc:Driver={Microsoft
Access Driver (*.mdb,
*.accdb)};DBQ=c:\\sagar\\emp.accdb;";

            Connection conn =
DriverManager.getConnection(database, "",
"");
            Statement s =
conn.createStatement();

            // create a table
```

```java
            String tableName = "myTable" +
String.valueOf((int)(Math.random() *
1000.0));
            String createTable = "CREATE
TABLE " + tableName +
                                  " (id
Integer, name Text(32))";
            s.execute(createTable);

            // enter value into table
            for(int i=0; i<25; i++)
            {
                String addRow = "INSERT INTO
" + tableName + " VALUES ( " +
                    String.valueOf((int)
(Math.random() * 32767)) + ", 'Text Value "
+

String.valueOf(Math.random()) + "')";
                s.execute(addRow);
            }

// read data from emp table;

    String selTable = "SELECT * FROM emp";
    s.execute(selTable);

        ResultSet rs = s.getResultSet();
        while((rs!=null) && (rs.next()))
            {

System.out.println(rs.getString(1) + " : "
+ rs.getString(2));

        }
            // drop the table
```

```
String dropTable = "DROP TABLE " +
tableName;
s.execute(dropTable);

        // close db
        s.close();
        conn.close();
    }
    catch(Exception ex)
    {
        ex.printStackTrace();
    }
```

9.9 Find the execution time in Java.

When executing test cases using selenium webdriver, we need to find the execution time of test cases. Below example illustrates how we can find the execution time in Java.

```
try{

long startTime =
System.currentTimeMillis();
// wait for 2 seconds

Thread.sleep(2000);

long elapsedTime =
System.currentTimeMillis() - startTime;

System.out.println("time diff in seconds: "
+ elapsedTime/1000);

}
```

```
catch(Exception ex)
{}
```

9.10 Sending mails in Java.

To be able to send email using gmail from Java, you will have to download javamail API library and add reference

https://java.net/projects/javamail/pages/Home

```
import javax.mail.*;
import javax.mail.internet.InternetAddress;
import javax.mail.internet.MimeMessage;
```

```
try
       {


final String fromEmail =
"autoemailrobot@gmail.com";
//gmail id

final String password = "xxx";
// password for gmail id

final String toEmail =
"reply2sagar@gmail.com";

Properties props = new Properties();

props.put("mail.smtp.host",
"smtp.gmail.com");
props.put("mail.smtp.port", "587");
```

```java
props.put("mail.smtp.auth", "true");
props.put("mail.smtp.starttls.enable",
"true");



Authenticator auth = new Authenticator() {
                protected
PasswordAuthentication
getPasswordAuthentication() {
                    return new
PasswordAuthentication(fromEmail,
password);
                }
            };

        Session session =
Session.getInstance(props, auth);

        MimeMessage msg = new
MimeMessage(session);
        //set message headers
        msg.addHeader("Content-type",
"text/HTML; charset=UTF-8");
        msg.addHeader("format",
"flowed");
        msg.addHeader("Content-Transfer-
Encoding", "8bit");

        msg.setFrom(new
InternetAddress("autoemailrobot@gmail.com",
"Automation Agent"));


msg.setReplyTo(InternetAddress.parse("autoe
mailrobot@gmail.com", false));
```

```java
        String subject ="Automation
resulst - pass - 10 Fail - 11";
        String body ="Reports";

        msg.setSubject(subject, "UTF-8");

        msg.setText(body, "UTF-8");

        msg.setSentDate(new Date());


msg.setRecipients(Message.RecipientType.TO,
InternetAddress.parse(toEmail, false));
        System.out.println("Send msg");
        Transport.send(msg);

    System.out.println("EMail Sent!");
        }
        catch (Exception e) {
          e.printStackTrace();
        }
```

10. Exception in Selenium Webdriver

In this chapter, you will learn how to handle exceptions that might occur while working with selenium webdriver in Java.

10.1 Exception handling in Java

There are 2 kinds of exceptions in Java. Checked and Unchecked Exceptions.

Checked Exceptions

The checked exceptions are exceptions that must be handled well before you execute your code. For example IOException is one such exception.

Unchecked Exceptions

The Unchecked exceptions are such exceptions that can occur at any time and we are not forced to handle these at compile-time.

Below example will illustrate how we can handle the exceptions in JAVA using try ... catch blocks.

```
try{

if (a / 0 == 2)
System.out.println("No exception occured");

}

catch(Exception ex){
System.out.println("exception occured" + ex.toString());
```

```
}
Finally{
System.out.println("Finally blocked is always executed");

}
```

Please remember that we can have many catch blocks after try block. Whenever exception occurs, it is thrown and caught by the catch block. In catch block we can write the code for recovery.

10.2 Exceptions in Selenium Webdriver

Below is the list of most commonly occuring exceptions When working with selenium webdriver.

1. ElementNotVisibleException
2. InvalidElementStateException
3. InvalidSelectorException
4. NoAlertPresentException
5. NoSuchElementException
6. NoSuchFrameException
7. NoSuchWindowException
8. StaleElementReferenceException
9. TimeoutException
10. UnhandledAlertException

Let us try to understand the meaning of each of these exceptions. We will also discuss on how to avoid these exceptions.

ElementNotVisibleException

This kind of exception occurs when the element you are trying to perform operation on is not visible. The style attribute – visibility of the element or it's parent is hidden.

To avoid this kind of exception, ensure that element is visible. If you are not able to make the element visible, try to execute javascript on that element.

```
WebElement we = driver.findElement(By.id("s"));

((JavascriptExecutor)
driver).executeScript("arguments[0].click();",w
e);
```

InvalidElementStateException

This kind of exception occurs when the element you are trying to perform operation on is in invalid state. There are many scenarios when this exception might occur.
For example Trying to invoke Clear() method on link will trigger this exception.
To avoid this exception, make sure that you are performing the correct operation on right element.

InvalidSelectorException

This kind of exception occurs when the xpath or css selector expression you are using to identify the element on the webpage is not correct by syntax.
For example – below statement will throw InvalidSelectorException

```
WebElement x =
driver.findElement(By.xpath("Images[:]"));
```

NoAlertPresentException

This kind of exception occurs when the element you are trying to switch the alert which is not present on web page.
To avoid this error, ensure that alert is really present on the webpage before switching to it.

NoSuchElementException

This kind of exception occurs when the findElement method is not able to find the element by the given identification method.
 To avoid this exception make sure that css or xpath expression you are using is correct. Also ensure that you are on right page and element is really loaded in the webpage. Some elements take longer time to load. So try to add synchronization points before trying to find them.

NoSuchFrameException

This kind of exception occurs when the frame you are trying to switch to does not exist.
To avoid this exception make sure that css or xpath expression you are using is correct. Also ensure that you are on right page and frame is really loaded in the webpage.

NoSuchWindowException

This kind of exception occurs when the window you are trying to switch to does not exist.

To avoid this exception make sure that window you are trying to switch is really open and window handle you are using is also correct.

StaleElementReferenceException

This kind of exception occurs when the element you trying to perform operation on is removed and re-added to the web page. This usually happens when ajax changes your page source asynchronously. In other words, A StaleElementException is thrown when the element you were interacting is destroyed and then recreated using ajax.When this happens the reference to the element in the DOM that you previously had becomes stale and you are no longer able to use this reference to interact with the element in the DOM. When this happens you will need to refresh your reference, or in real world terms find the element again.

To avoid this exception, try to find the element again and again until you do not get StaleElementReferenceException.

TimeoutException

This kind of exception occurs when you use `WebDriverWait` to wait for some element.

UnhandledAlertException

This kind of exception occurs when alert is present on the webpage and you are trying to perform some operation on elements on the webpage.

11. Excel Programming in SELENIUM

> *In this chapter, you will learn how to read and write microsoft excel files in Java using apache POI library.*

Apache POI (http://poi.apache.org) provides the Java library to work with Microsoft excel workbooks.

11.1 Creating and writing data to Excel Workbook

When we design a test automation framework in Selenium, we usually store the test data inside excel sheets.

Below example demonstrates how we can create and write to excel workbook.

```java
public class Excel
{
        public static void main(String[] args)
        {

XSSFWorkbook workbook = new XSSFWorkbook();
//Create a blank sheet

XSSFSheet worksheet =
workbook.createSheet("xyz");

Row row = worksheet.createRow(0);

Cell cell = row.createCell(0);
```

```
cell.setCellValue("hi");

try
        {

        //Write the workbook on disk

FileOutputStream out = new FileOutputStream(new

File("newwb.xlsx"));

workbook.write(out);

out.close();

        }
        catch (Exception e)
        {
                e.toString();
        }
}   //main method body ends

} //class ends
```

11.2 Reading data from existing workbook

We can read the data from excel sheets using below code.

```
try
   {
//open workbook

FileInputStream file = new FileInputStream(new
File("newwb.xlsx"));

XSSFWorkbook workbook = new XSSFWorkbook(file);
```

```java
//access desired worksheet
XSSFSheet worksheet = workbook.getSheetAt(0);

Iterator<Row> rowIterator =
worksheet.iterator();

//loop through all rows in given worksheet

while (rowIterator.hasNext())
    {

 Row row = rowIterator.next();


Iterator<Cell> cellIterator =
row.cellIterator();

    //loop through all the column cells for
given row

                while (cellIterator.hasNext())
                {
                    Cell cell =
cellIterator.next();

//based upon the data type of cell, use
appropriate method

            switch (cell.getCellType())
            {
  case Cell.CELL_TYPE_NUMERIC:
  System.out.print(cell.getNumericCellValue());
  break;
  case Cell.CELL_TYPE_STRING:
  System.out.print(cell.getStringCellValue());
  break;
                }
            }
                System.out.println("-Next Row
Starts-");
```

```
            }

//close file after reading all cell values

        file.close();

    } //try ends

    catch (Exception e)
    {
        e.toString();
    }
```

12. Framework Designing in SELENIUM

In this chapter, you will learn about variuos automation testing frameworks in Selenium. You will also learn about how to design the keyword driven automation framework in Java.

There are 3 types of automation frameworks that can be designed in selenium. Please note that In any other automation tools like QTP, Winrunner similar kinds of frameworks are popular.

12.1 Data Driven Framework

In data driven framework, importance is given to test data than multiple functionality of application. We design data driven framework to work with applications where we want to test same flow with different test data.

12.2 Hybrid Framework

This is the combination of keyword and data driven frameworks.
After analyzing the application, you can decide what kind of framework best suits your needs and then you can design automation framework in SELENIUM.

12.3 Keyword Driven Framework

In Keyword Driven Framework , Importance is given to functions than Test Data. when we have to test multiple functionality we can go for keyword frameworks. Each keyword is mapped to function in SELENIUM library and application.

Components of Keyword Driven framework

Keyword driven Automation Framework is most popular test automation framework. It is very easy to design and learn a keyword driven automation framework in SELENIUM.

In this article I will explain you all details about how we can design and use keyword driven automation framework in SELENIUM with example. I will also explain the advantages and disadvantages of keyword driven automation framework in SELENIUM.
In keyword driven automation framework, focus is mainly on kewords/functions and not the test data. This means we focus on creating the functions that are mapped to the functionality of the application.

For example - Suppose you have a flight reservation application which provides many features like

1. Login to the application

2. Search Flights

3. Book Flight tickets

4. Cancel Tickets

5. Fax Order

6. View Reports

To implement the keyword driven automation framework for this kind of application we will create functions in Java for each functionality mentioned above. We pass the test data and test object details to these functions.

The main components of keyword driven automation framework in SELENIUM

Each keyword driven automation framework has some common components as mentioned below.

1. Scripts Library

2. Test Data (generally in excel format)

3. SELENIUM - Settings and Environment Variables

4. Reports - (Generally in HTML format)

5. Test Driver Script Method

Test Data Sheet in keyword driven framework in SELENIUM.

Generally automated test cases are stored in excel sheets. From SELENIUM script ,we read excel file and then row by row we execute the functions in a test case. Each test case is implemented as a set of keywords.

Common columns in Data sheet are mentioned below.

1. Test case ID - Stores the Test Case ID mapped to Manual Test Cases.

2. Test Case Name - Name of the Test cases/ Scenario.

3. Execute Flag - if Marked Y -> Test case will be executed

4. Test_Step_Id - Steps in a test case

5. Keyword - Mapped to function in library file.

6. Object Types - Class of the object e.g winedit, webedit, swfbutton etc

7. Object Names -Names of objects in OR .

8. Object Values - Actual test data to be entered in the objects.

9. Parameter1 - This is used to control the execution flow in the function.

Test_ID	TC_Name	Execute	Test_Step_ID	Keyword	Object_Types	Object_Names	Object_Values	Parameter1
1	Login To App	Y	Step1	login	winedit;winedit	userid;password	salunke;mercury	
			Step2	Insert_Order	wincombobox;wincombobo	flyfrom;flyto	london;paris	
			Step3	Fax_Order				Order_Id

Please note that this is just a sample data sheet that can be used in keyword driven framework. There could be customized data sheets for each project depending upon the requirement and design.

For example there could be more parameters or test data is stored in the databases.

Test Driver Script in SELENIUM.

This is the heart of keyword driven / data driven frameworks. This is the main script that interacts with all modules mentioned above.

Main tasks that are accomplished by driver script are ->

1. Read data from the Environment variables.

2. Call report module to create Report folders / files

3. Read Excel file

4. Call the function mapped to keyword.

5. Log the result

13. Miscellaneous topics on SELENIUM

In this chapter, you will get to know about selenium IDE, Selenium Grid and Junit. You will also learn about multi-browser testing, challenges and limitations of Selenium Webdriver.

13.1 Selenium IDE.

Selenium IDE is a Firefox plugin which records and plays back user interactions with the browser. Use this to either create simple scripts or assist in exploratory testing. You can also export the test scripts in languages like Java, C#, Ruby and Python.

You can install Selenium IDE xpi file from
http://release.seleniumhq.org/selenium-ide/

Follow below steps to install Selenium IDE

1. Open firefox browser
2. Go to tools -> Add-ons
3. Click on Gear icon ->Install add on from file
4. Browse xpi file downloaded from selenium site
5. Click on install now and restart Firefox

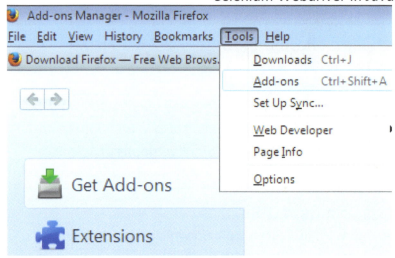

Figure 18 - Open Add-Ons page in Firefox

Click on the gear icon and then select Install Add-on From File...

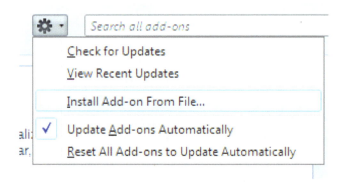

Figure 19 - Install Add-on from file

Then Browse to the selenium IDE xpi file downloaded from selenium website and select it. You will see next image.

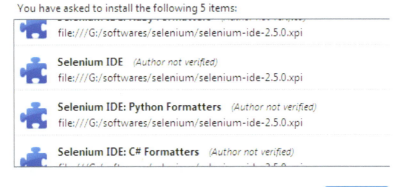

Figure 20 - Install Selenium IDE add on

After you click on Install Now button, Add-on will be installed and you will have to restart the firefox. Then you will have to go to the Tools -> Selenium IDE to start it.

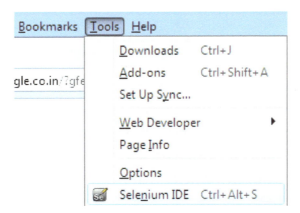

Figure 21 - Launch Selenium IDE in firefox

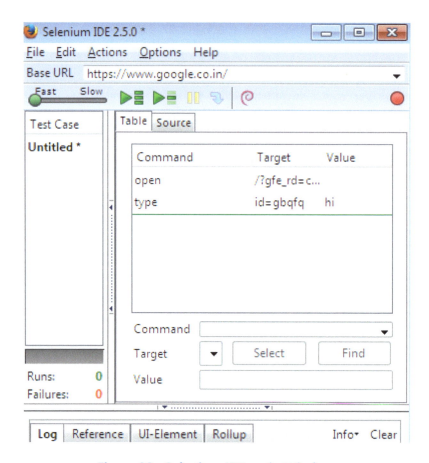

Figure 22 - Selenium IDE main Window

When you open selenium IDE, recording is automatically started. You can perform any operation on the web page open in firefox browser. As you can see in previuos figure, It shows the commands as we record it. We can export the test case in many languages as shown in next figure.

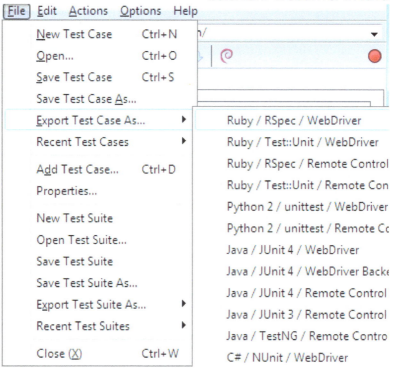

Figure 23 - Export test case in various languages

13.2 Selenium Grid.

Selenium Grid is used for running tests in parallel on different machines(called as nodes) from central machine(called as Hub).

Hub acts as a cental server. Based upon the configuration of the nodes (browser , OS), Hub will select the node and trigger the execution.

13.3 Junit Testing Framework in Selenium.

Junit is a unit testing framework developed in Java. It is mainly used by developers to test the code. Junit is mainly used for white box testing.

As a functional tester, we should use keyword driven framework.

13.3 Multi-Browser Testing using Selenium.

Selenium webdriver is very popular tool to test cross-browser compatibility of the web applications.

The code you write for one browser say Firefox can be used as it is for other browsers like Internet Explorer, Chrome, Safari etc.

13.4 Limitations of Selenium Webdriver.

Below is the list of limitation of selenium.
1. Selenium webdriver only supports testing of web applications.
2. Desktop based applications developed in Java and .Net can not be automated using Selenium Webdriver
3. We can not automate or verify the Flash Content, Silverlight Apps , Applet Contents using Selenium Webdriver.

www.ingramcontent.com/pod-product-compliance
Lightning Source LLC
Chambersburg PA
CBHW041143050326

40689CB00001B/461